Is Bitcoin Bull$h!t?

I0002160

Contents

Prologue

I set out to do a few things with this book. First, let me say that the book was not originally a book, and spawned from an article written for a cryptocurrency website called "The Coin Front" that was sold and is no longer owned by the same people as when I wrote for them. I will give a quick backstory into how this came to be.

A writer for the Coin Front put out an article about the potential of cryptocurrency early in 2014, and I had a few disagreements with their perspectives about the possibilities, so I reached out to them. The author responded by inviting me to pen an open response which would be published in the Coin Front as a direct response to the original article.

The article I originally wrote was well-received by the audience and the team, so we came to the agreement that I would turn my original article into an eight-part series analyzing cryptocurrency relative to the "gold rush" to compare and contrast at a high level two potentially similar economic events. I published the articles over time, taking care to research each article painstakingly in depth, even if the outcome was a relatively brief writing.

In the course of putting out these articles, I started to get more work in the blockchain space between writing articles and working on projects in various capacities. As I had previous experience in coding as well as team building, I decided to take an academic and critical look at the blockchain space to aide my work in the area. I had a problem with how academia seemed to analyze industries from the outside, and wanted to do something about it. I decided to start trying to tread the middle ground between being an academic and being a professional in the field. I wanted to get the best of both worlds and synthesize them into my work.

In this, I wanted this piece to become a conversation between history, my work, my experience, and the market. In the process, I developed what I called "Decentralized Conglomerate Theory" and wrote a white paper for OpenLedger. There are many things that led me to come up with DCT, but the biggest event that led me to this was covering the North American Bitcoin Conference in Chicago. It was at this event I originally heard Vitalik Buterin present a theoretical framework for the "Decentralized Autonomous Organization". Many people were floored and amazed by his framework, but as I sat in the audience taking notes, some glaring problems jumped out to me.

To this day I still have the notes I took from that event, because not only did I use them as the basis for a new theory, I knew when I was taking the notes that I had struck upon something that was potentially paradigm shifting. Now, I would not be satisfied with these theories staying on paper, and ended up working with OpenLedger on developing their digital infrastructure around DCT.

As of this writing, OpenLedger seems to be thriving and doing well using DCT, however I am not working with them and have not been working with them for various reasons which I will get into in the epilogue. There are certain things that the readers will not be able to understand in the prologue that necessitate reading the body of the book to understand why I will save the discussion of these subjects for the epilogue.

What to me began as an experiment in bridging real world market dynamics and academic study, I also began to learn about harsh realities that I did not truly understand before this grand adventure.

On a slightly different note, I REALLY hate the flow of academic writing. I do not believe I am the only one that has disdain for the broken flow of footnotes and citations that are necessary for proving a point academically. This is my book, so I'm not going to write academically because I don't have to. I feel like by the end, the reader will thank me for this. As well, in 2019, anything that I say can easily be fact-checked. It's tiresome and redundant for me to put in a citation that someone will inevitably try to fact check and debunk anyway, so let the debunkers do the footnotes and citing for me. I put sources at the end as proof for pretty much everything I said, but as far as putting in citations and footnotes...fuck all that...

So here we are dear reader...I have given you a brief introduction to what you're about to read, so you understand why it started in 2014 and didn't finish until 2019. This was an organically written work. This is a living conversation with the market. It is only my perspective, but I put my life and soul into this book. Now, this is yours to do with it what you will, whether it is to gain knowledge or simply for entertainment.

SECTION 1:

From the Gold Coin to the Bit Coin

TLDR: The average person doesn't know how 80% of the things they use daily work, but as long as society benefits, it doesn't matter.

PUNCH: Modern Humanity is an illusion, and the average human is useless without google or wikipedia.

Chapter 1 - The Paradox of a Unilateral Currency

There is a growing divide in the crypto-currency community about whether it is better to have Bitcoin be the one coin that represents the entire community, or if the current trend of new alternative coins is good for the crypto-ecosystem long term.

TLDR: Bitcoin Maximalism V.S. diverse alternative ecosystems

PUNCH: Bitcoin is a cult

Some arguments for using only Bitcoin are that too many coins dilute the buying power of the crypto-currency community at large, and that having too many coins makes it impossible to keep track of for the user. On the other hand, the arguments for alternative currencies are based around having more representation for minority groups, allowing special interests to pool their resources on a worldwide scale, and allowing the currency holder to decide what interests their currency supports.

In order to accurately understand the potential impact of either scenario, we need to first disambiguate the idea of a "currency" vs. the idea of a "commodity"

Currencies and commodities are consumed, used, and traded on a daily basis by almost everyone living in modern society. Despite this fact, these are two of the most commonly misunderstood concepts in of one of the most capitalistic societies on Earth, the United States of America.

For this reason, before moving any further into the topic of crypto-currencies, let's review the Merriam Webster Dictionary's definitions of these two terms.

cur•ren•cy

(1) the money that a country uses :

(2) a specific kind of money

: something that is used as money

: (3) the quality or state of being used or accepted by many people

com•mod•i•ty

(1) something that is bought and sold

(2) something or someone that is useful or valued

While both currency and commodity are clearly two different entities with completely different functions and purposes within modern economies, their paths merge in the world of crypto currency. That's been the case with Bitcoin.

But before we dive into the new and novel, let's get a better grasp of the current global economy.

What is a "currency" and how does it function?

Ultimately, a currency serves as a ledger. It's a way to measure trade consistently.

In a barter system, the metric for value is determined between the parties involved in the trade. In other words, If you have a loaf of bread and I have a bunch of kale and we trade them, that loaf of bread is worth one bunch of kale because of our agreement.

In a "currency" system, a community establishes a common value that is recognized throughout the community.

An obvious example of this would be the U.S. Dollar. There are 50 states in the U.S. which all operate based around the U.S. Dollar. On the surface this seems trivial, since most countries use the same currency across their territory. But the United States has many micro-economies within its borders.

Take a look at the cost of an apartment in New York City and in Indianapolis, for example.

According to Numbeo.com, it takes $6,437 a month to live at the same standard which $3,300 a month would buy you in Indianapolis.

The average income in New York is higher than it is in Indianapolis, but when you factor in the cost of living it's not extra income, just a reflection of the higher cost of living in that city. It's obvious that the US dollar doesn't have a consistent value there.

When examining the wealth disparity among micro-economies in the U.S. the disparity seems to be regulated by the locality. So if your costs are higher, your pay is generally higher.

This is true within the borders of the United States. However, when a US citizen from New York and a citizen from Indianapolis decide to go to France, then they both have to use the U.S. dollar to buy Euros. Quickly, the citizen from Indiana loses the sense of "equal" buying power because the disparate economies within the US give the person from New York City more USD for doing the same work.

When both of these citizens exit their local economies, they are using the same currency, but they received the currencies from different pay scales. Of course, no one in France cares about this when exchanging the dollar into Euros. It is not a "New York" dollar, or an "Indiana" dollar. It's just a dollar.

Ultimately, a currency has a value within a micro-economy (on a local level) and a value within a macro-economy (on a national level).

What's the Solution?

One solution that has come about to solving the disparate economy problem is having localized currencies.

What this does is allow a micro-community to establish their own currency that goes farther within the community than the macro-currency, allowing the community to keep capital local, and not have the macro-currency drain it into international corporations or even into different states where the taxes do not contribute to local infrastructure.

This has been taken even further to have currency specific to one store or one commodity. There are time based currencies, which allows a person to trade currency for labor, and there are commodity based currencies, the most well-known being the gold standard.

But commodities and currencies are not mutually exclusive. A coin made out of gold is both a commodity and a currency if it is traded. But in the face of increased globalization and centralization, most countries have abandoned commodity based currencies for fiat currency. This ties the currency to their macro-economy.

While this system is in place to help the macro-economy have better long term stability, the major problem is the centralization of authority over resources. Having a centralized currency puts the control of the resource mobility in the hands of whoever controls the currency.

In the case of the United States, the resources are controlled by the banking system. The government provides tax funded subsidies to corporations to invest in the infrastructure of the United States. This is the principle of trickle-down economics. The centralization is part of the governing mechanism.

While trickle-down economics is nothing new, the recent development of crypto-currencies poses a threat to the centralized monetary system, and a major component of that is the variety of currencies being developed.

Currently, the most widely accepted crypto-currency is Bitcoin.

While Bitcoin is very much being used as a currency, it is also being traded like a commodity. Investors have seen arbitrage opportunities that exist with crypto-currencies, and they have taken advantage of them. This was standard practice with international currencies until laws made the profit not worth the time of arbitrage.

Since most "crypto-currencies" are not actually accepted for trade, they're considered commodities. Many crypto-traders treat coins as penny stocks, and simply see them as opportunities for arbitrage. It is important to note that just because something is called a "crypto-currency" it does not actually mean it is a "currency".

When talking about free-market economic theories, one cannot help but see the current state of crypto-currencies as the closest manifestation to a "free market" that has ever been seen on a global scale.

Crypto-currencies have allowed us the capacity to trade between borders under the same currency, and also to develop currencies that have a global interest at the root of their cause. Great examples of this are Potcoin, Rainbowcoin, and Marinecoin. If you look at the purpose statements of each of these currencies, they have intentions to use resources on a global scale to affect change.

Potcoin is aiming to be a commodity backed coin that allows users to purchase legal cannabis with it. If you live in the United States, you can use US Dollars to support legalization groups, but in the process actively using USD contributes to an economy that prosecutes cannabis smokers federally, and switching to Potcoin not only allows a person to not contribute to that system, but it puts resources towards legalizing cannabis on a global scale.

The same is true for Rainbowcoin. It is very easy for an American citizen to use USD to support activism to help the LGBT community, but in the process, they still are supporting the very government that has been legislating that they are second class citizens. Putting resources into Rainbowcoin allows people to actively avoid paying to persecute themselves, as a member of the LGBT community must pay taxes in America, while not enjoying the same protections and rights as a non-LGBT American.

Marinecoin is even more different than the aforementioned currencies, because as an entity, Marinecoin is trying to build an actual eco-system that supports the currency, and also use hashing power to compute equations that will solve real-world problems, such as genome sequencing, cancer research, and basically anything that can be broken down into variables. Marinecoin is working to become an actual "currency" and not just another penny-stock commodity.

While these three coins have very different goals, strategies, and methods of execution, ultimately they serve as resource repositories. A group of people has decided to pool their resources towards one goal. Crypto-currencies are allowing special interest groups to connect with each other on a global scale and pool their resources together, whether computing power, or actual currency. One currency will not, and CAN NOT, represent 7 billion people.

Chapter 2 - How Can Cryptocurrency Move Forward?

If there is one thing that almost everyone in the crypto world has in common, it is the loss of money through scams or larceny. The bad, the ugly, and the worst.

Without science, capitalism is simply people trying to come up with new methods of stealing.

Whether it is a pump and dump, an attack on an exchange, or a long con, it has been nearly impossible to remain unscathed in the free market of the crypto economy. With new regulations on the horizon from the US government concerning tax laws, many crypto users are looking at the potential to have their currency taxed not only for the coming years, but also retroactively.

What has NOT been discussed, however, is any protection for cryptos. It seems governments want to take money from the crypto communities through taxation, but they want to leave us to fend for ourselves. Who can the crypto community trust to protect it from the scammers and thieves?

To better understand this dilemma, we should examine why "trust" is fundamentally at the basis of a functional community.

In social scientist Francis Fukuyama's book, Trust: The Social Virtues and The Creation of Prosperity(1996), he presents the following argument: at the basis of every functional society, trust must exist, and even further the more trust a society has, the easier it is for that society to create prosperity.

To summarize, Fukuyama posits that a society with laws can function not just because of the laws, but because people trust the laws will be enforced, so things like ownership and legal contracts become possible because people invest their own trust in the system.

He makes the case that it's easier to create a large consolidated firm in a place where there is more trust. He also mentions that in light of new technology, people would be able to connect on smaller scales and create firms that were not based around countries or local economies, but also functioned on the trust between individuals. In essence, it is the trust that allows firms to work as a unit towards the same goal.

While it's not easy to accurately measure trust, it's easy to see that trust in the crypto world is fading, and it is mainly due to the scammers and thieves, not because of the systems themselves.

Since the crypto world is largely based around anonymity, our first level of trust is gone. We don't know the names or faces of people we are dealing with. Such a simple gesture goes a long way in establishing trust, but not many people in the crypto world want to take that first step.

Now that we know that many countries will not only tax crypto, but they will not actively protect them, another level of trust is gone, which would have been the legal system to protect this realm.

But the worst thing affecting trust now, is the thieves and scammers themselves. While these types are not unique to the crypto world, since this technology is so early in its inception, they have the potential to cause mass distrust in the crypto world and cause it to fall apart.

With the current state of the crypto economy, we are all faced with a choice. Do we retreat to what feels safe, and what we feel we can trust in the old legal system and old currency, or do we band together as individuals and force the thieves out on our own since the governments will not and cannot do it?

The crypto world is the Wild West. We have no Wyatt Earp, so we must all be the sheriff.

Chapter 3 - A New Wave of Pioneers: Mining the Unknown

The comparison of the Crypto Rush to the Gold Rush has been made on numerous occasions over the past years. It's clearly the most appropriate comparison, both metaphorically, and literally.

TLDR: The profit around every rush comes from selling dreams

Punch: There's no such thing as scarcity

Unfortunately, many of the people who compared cryptocurrency to gold have pessimistic views on crypto's future— plagued with an inability to see beyond the looming threat of taxation from the US government and threat of Russian and Chinese bans on their official use in commerce.

For once, these three superpowers agree on something. Unfortunately, it's their dislike of Bitcoin.

For some speculators/economists, these government attitudes signal the end of the Crypto Rush. When these speculators/economists attempt to draw parallels between the Crypto Rush and the historic Gold Rush, they are engaging in the age-old exercise of actively and knowingly cherry picking their comparisons to bolster their argument.

But if we compare the current state of cryptocurrency to the Gold Rush's economic impact, we can see the potential cryptocurrency has. The rapid innovation taking place within cryptocurrency communities may make the Industrial Revolution look like a trivial episode in the world of technological and economic development.

This is the first in an eight-part series on how cryptocurrencies relate to the past, and how they can help shape the future. We'll discuss the concerns around the current Crypto Rush, demonstrate how it can bring the same economic and technological benefits the Gold Rush did more than a century ago, and describe the relationship between coin developers (coders), miners, panhandlers (the people getting free coins), and merchants in the cryptocurrency world.

The History of The Gold Rush

Let's start with the history of the Gold Rush and establish context for why the Crypto Rush has so much potential for economic change.

California, one of the most prosperous and densely populated states in the union, owes a part of that to the Gold Rush. San Francisco, for example, grew from around <u>1,000 people to more than 20,000</u> within only two years.

Most of these people were gold prospectors, looking to earn their fortune. But as more and more people arrived, it became harder and harder to find <u>gold</u>. If you were serious about it, you needed better technology.

While the big investors were able to afford hydraulic drills, that <u>didn't</u> <u>stop panhandlers</u> from making the potential six-month trek in hopes of getting rich.

Ultimately, tensions over increasing scarcity came to a head when miners from China started showing up in California for gold too, and consequently a "foreigner's tax" was imposed.

Who Gets Richest From Mining? It's Not The Miners...

Miners aside, though, the long term economic implications of the Gold Rush lie in the fact that the merchants who set up shop around the miners were the same people to walk away with the most profits from the era.

While the miners put the most effort and energy into retrieving the gold from the Earth, the driving reason they did it was so they could have capital and be able to purchase tangible items or pay for manpower.

With gold, a person could get a house built, buy a cow, or simply buy more mining equipment. The gold rush for a short time was an ecosystem driven by the miners, but once the gold ran out, the merchants were left with the gold and with thriving businesses.

What Does This Have To Do With The Crypto Rush?

Besides these more obvious parallels, new adaptations to mining are happening today as a direct result of the Crypto Rush.

I speak, of course, of the ever-changing mining hardware that miners use as a result of the competitive environment of the crypto-currency world. A preliminary list of the different mining hardware types can help illustrate the often convoluted intricacies of the field of mining-tools (digital pick-axes, if you will):CPU, GPU, FPGA, ASIC, Cloud, and proxy by contract.

Some of the hardware has become obsolete, while other hardware resurged from obsolescence. The mining community doesn't take well to drastic changes in hardware, but that's mostly because of the obvious loss of investment that comes with obsolete technology.

The miners want to be compensated for their investment and their energy input, but since the companies that create the hardware are not vested in any one coin, they try to make their hardware work for as many coins as possible.

This causes some friction between the mining communities, the exchange communities, the hardware companies, and the developers. For example, look at the large number of ASIC resistant coins that came about from the desire to take the advantage away from ASIC mining machines.

This doesn't keep hardware developers from wanting to capitalize off these increasingly frequent hardware arms races, though, and in turn they make

hardware that can mine the aforementioned ASIC resistant coins.

The new hardware then perpetuates the so called "fair distribution"

communities and new forms of distribution are invented to overcome

inevitable hardware changes. While this friction may cause hiccups in the

short term relationship between the miners, merchants, and panhandlers,

the constant attempts to make improvements will cause progress to happen

at an unprecedented rate.

The crypto-currency world is full of ebbs and flows of resistance and

improvement, but everyone is looking to make progress. Thus, while miners

don't like to see their hardware become obsolete, that sudden obsolescence

usually signifies a new major development in mining hardware or

cryptocurrency software. This cumulative advancement will contribute to

greater long-term effects unimaginable in an environment dictated by the

simultaneous desire for economic stasis and the potential for personal

wealth.

In the next part of this series, we will take a more in depth look at the mining equipment to see how the Crypto Rush moved from pick-axes to hydraulic drills, and what that implication means for the Crypto Rush.

Chapter 4 - A New Hope: From The Industrial Revolution To The Age Of Machines

In this continuation of our series covering the Crypto Rush, we take a look at the rapid changes in mining technology, and how market speculators influenced both the price of gold and the development of the various technologies used to mine it.

Technology evolves too fast for humans to keep up.

Humans are dependant on technology, and simultaneously hate that we're dependant on technology.

The impact of speculators on the value of gold highlights another important facet of the Gold Rush which parallels the Crypto Rush: access to fast and reliable communication. In both cases information gaps became opportunities for arbitrage or exploitation.

Speculation, technological innovation, and communication are all major factors affecting the transition into the machine age as a whole. The sudden injection of capital, new technology, and better communication not only built local economies, but quickened the pace of global economic development.

Looking at the evolution of mining hardware, it's easy to see the sharp spike in development, and a decline in progress that was just as rapid. Both the mining equipment industry and the market for gold went through a similar boom and bust, and what they had in common were the speculators themselves.

As common people became interested in investing to make money, they injected more capital into the speculator's market. In some cases the speculator's market left people with a valuable commodity like gold, but in other cases they ended up with pyrite, or fool's gold. Pyrite is hardly useless, but it's more common and less stable than gold.

Eventually, The Gold Rush hit the point at which the speculators began to exhaust the gold deposits, which meant the mining equipment development became less profitable. As a result, a stark division showed up in the gold markets: a speculator's market and a utility market.

The utility market employed gold as plating for transistors and wiring, while the speculators' market hoarded gold bars and coins. On the surface it may appear that the speculator's market might not have had merit, but in the transition from the industrial to the machine age, these gold stores would fund the utility market. This would fuel a completely new wave of technology that didn't exist before the massive gold mines were discovered.

One of the main ways that speculators drained capital from the economy was by their exploitation of information gaps. During that era, methods of communication varied to the point that one party could receive information sometimes months in advance of other parties. Whether it was selling mining equipment or dumping gold on the market because a new larger store had been discovered, this information gap was used by speculators to time their buying and selling decisions in order to exploit both sides. The shorter the information gap became, the smaller the window was for arbitrage

opportunities; and this continues to be the case with the Crypto Rush as well.

In essence, the speculators either make bigger gambles in the smaller

windows or become less of a drain due to smaller opportunity. But if we

consider the speculators to be economic drains, we may be overlooking their

ability to inject capital into the utilitarian market.

Keynesian economics has framed this concept as "trickledown" economics,

but their theoretical approach has not only been proven wrong by history,

but the school of thermo-economics shows the Keynesian system to be

unsustainable long term because of speculators draining capital.

The framework of thermo-economics applies the laws of thermo-dynamics to

the economy, and in the case of speculators, this construct would deem that

speculators cause entropy to occur in economic systems.

The speculators' market is not a problem inherently, but when that market

overtakes the utility market which actually makes products, the speculators

drain too much of the energy from the market bringing it to a gradual halt

over time.

Conversely, if technology progresses too fast in one area and not in its related areas, it causes an overload in the microsystem. This means that new technology is created faster than it can be fully turned into a commodity or a tool to make commodities.

One of history's best examples is William Murdoch's steam locomotive, which he invented in 1784. His invention changed the course of transportation, but it had to be timed with the placement of a proper infrastructure for progress to happen on a micro and macro scale, and that didn't happen until nearly fifty years later.

In essence, when the principles of thermo-economics are applied to the Crypto Rush, we can demonstrate this phenomenon's potential to instigate a major technological leap forward due to the new and increased injection of capital and resources into the economic system.

Thus, rather than letting speculators drive technological development and drain crucial amounts of energy from the entire system, they have to be put to use in the crypto-economy as a necessary overload-prevention mechanism.

In the next part of the series, we'll take a look at the machine age further by exploring how it differed from the industrial age, and what its relationship is to modern times. While the Gold Rush initially was about the gold itself, the further consequences of that era were a major jump in transistor and computational processing efficiency to such an advanced degree that it allowed humans to land on the moon.

Chapter 5 - The Empire Strikes Back: Broadcasting a Corporate Takeover

The Gold Rush was an ideal parallel historical reference point to begin our exploration of today's Crypto Rush. However, as with the Gold Rush, the story does not end when the gold extraction ends, but instead continues through the markets, corporations, inventions, and innovations fueled by the Gold Rush.

The beginning of the crypto rush was the teenage years, now Crypto has to put on a suit and grow up.

Crypto has to move out of its mom's basement

Thus, we can expect similar developments as a result of the Crypto Rush. As the Gold Rush died down, new corporations emerged in a market that was flooded with capital, innovation, and an unprecedented level of connectivity. The completion of massive railroad, telecommunications, and banking systems in a relatively short window of time created a perfect storm of capital and opportunity to propel the U.S. economy into an epoch that dwarfed the productivity and innovation of the industrial revolution of the eighteenth and nineteenth centuries.

As mentioned in previous articles, one of the major effects of the Gold Rush was the increased need for long distance communication. The Pony Express was created in 1860 specifically to deliver mail and information between the east coast, the south, and the increasingly populated west coast. It took an average of ten days for a message or package to be delivered from one coast to the other.

While the Pony Express played a major role in this period in American history, its existence was short lived. The Introduction of the telegraph system was such a major innovation that it took only two days to put the Pony Express out of business after the new communications system successfully connected the two disparate coasts on October 24, 1861.

In the short period between 1848 and 1861, the United States went from using horse drawn postal carriers to a telegraph system that carried correspondences coast to coast. This cut idle waiting time down from ten days to mere minutes/hours.

With this improvement a new sense of technological possibility captivated the public. As a result of this fascination, innovators were often boosted to celebrity status. Inventors like Thomas Edison (often referred to as the "Wizard of Menlo Park") used their public influence, capital, and inventions to thereafter shape the technological landscape of the United States. This is not to be confused with so-called "robber barons" who were considered to exploitative by the public at large.

With so many technological advancements happening at the same time, less wealthy individuals gained unprecedented access to communication and transportation technology. While these systems were owned by a small group of people, they were created to serve the entire country.

And as the infrastructure became better, more people were able to find decent jobs, and more people came to America. The economic boom that came along with this technological progress meant better banking institutions were needed to manage the growing volume of capital.

As the transportation, communication, and banking institutions settled into their new environments a dynamic economy emerged. The interplay of these industries allowed the macro economy to flourish, as a symbiotic existence allowed all parties involved to benefit from this mutual existence.

In the context of the Crypto Rush, systems like Maidsafe or Ethereum might represent similar emerging infrastructures as they seek to decentralize the internet itself from service providers and government control. In trying to support the cryptocurrency economy, the coming systems will likely be as dramatic a shift as going from the Pony Express to a coast to coast telegraph system.

In the same way that the introduction of file sharing changed how media is distributed, the Crypto Rush has the potential to change the way capital is distributed. Just as the communication and banking infrastructures benefited from the Gold Rush, if the proper complementary systems are flourishing during the Crypto Rush, a dynamic economy will emerge and thrust the macro economy into a more advanced stage which we can call "Proto-Dynamism".

In the next part of the series, the importance of regulation will be addressed, as we examine the historical bank runs that led to the Great Depression.

Chapter 6 - Return of the Jedi: Using the Force of Regulation

One of the major issues facing the Crypto Rush is the looming threat of regulation into obsolescence. As China and Russia threaten to ban Bitcoin, and the United States threatens to tax it into oblivion, the former free market is being shaken by the impending possibilities of government crackdowns.

Regulatory bodies will not allow themselves to be usurped.

You can't have leaders telling you that it's going to be a leaderless movement.

(A leader in a movement about an ideology that claims leaderless

systems is a hypocrite)

While some cryptocurrency enthusiasts think regulation will ultimately be the death of cryptocurrency, some parts of the community believe some level of regulation is necessary to save the currencies from thieves and hackers with bad intentions.

One can look to history to get an example of the extreme sides of under-regulating, and conversely what happens when something is over-regulated. In one case, under-regulation led to the Great Depression and in another case over regulation led to the United States government effectively stealing gold from its citizens.

Following the Gold Rush, a speculators' market emerged where gold was bought and sold in expectation of profits based on the rising demand and fading supply.

While many of these trades were legitimate, there were many con artists who passed off pyrite as gold, and plated metals like lead with a layer of gold to trick buyers into paying exorbitant prices for relatively worthless items. As more people were taken advantage of in schemes that extended beyond just selling fool's gold, government intervention seemed to be the only resolution to protecting the citizens. To properly contextualize regulation surrounding the Gold Rush, we should briefly examine the regulation and deregulation that occurred before it.

Central banking was first established in America in 1790, but due to war and unforeseen economic distresses, it became insolvent, and new charters were made to establish a second central bank to try to salvage previous investments.

In the middle of the economic crises, the brief War of 1812 caused economic stresses on all sides and increased tensions between the Americans and the British. The war was heavily focused around the trade blockades Britain had put up around France, as the Americans and French established a diplomatic relationship with the Louisiana Purchase.

The disputes between Britain and France in turn affected the British and American relations. With British charters eventually being cut off, and post war debts mounting, the banking system in America fell apart, leaving the citizens to re-establish the localized economies that existed with colonial currencies. This would be a perfect storm for allowing the Gold Rush to emerge in a near free market so the economy could be re-established without too much regulation stifling the market.

Retrospectively, the period from 1800-1848 may be observed as a battle for resources. The American government annexed the oil rich Texas from The Republic of Mexico, and established American sovereignty in California following the conclusion of the Mexican-American War. Consequently, the influx of newly found capital from gold, and the subsequent discoveries of large oil reserves in Texas in 1894 was the perfect environment for giant corporate conglomerates to form unchecked by any governing body.

Leading up to the turn of the century, the railroad system began to make national trade much easier and became the backbone of the American economic infrastructure. In 1887 the Interstate Commerce Act established a means to regulate private corporations because of the railroad industry's increased power through monopolization.

Initially this act was aimed directly at the railroad industry, but the act extended beyond just railroad companies. The Department of Commerce and

Labor was formed in 1903 to prevent corporations from abusing their workers in the same vein as the 1887 act was meant to protect consumers and workers alike.

With the influx of new capital, and increased regulation on speculation, it was only a matter of time before this culture would spread into the banking system. As investment funds became heavily concentrated, the chances of massive gains increased, but so did the chances for devastating losses.

This speculative cycle nearly collapsed the economy in the Panic of 1907 following heavy stock market manipulation and a resulting bank run, but J.P. Morgan effectively united a group of banks and saved the failing economy from the lost capital drained by bad speculation, bad banking practices, and empty promises made by con artists posing as legitimate businesses.

In an attempt to re-establish a central banking authority and prevent another economic disaster, the Federal Reserve Act established a new system of banks that would hold assets in an attempt to ensure the country could have asset backed solvency.

This act would start a series of extremely polarized decisions by the federal government concerning involvement in private sector ventures. As the new central banking system began to establish itself alongside the stock market, rampant speculation and scam artists led to a bank run and market crash that thrust America into the Great Depression.

The federal government then passed the Glass Steagall Act to try and prevent large banking conglomerates from mixing commercial and investment banking. The point of this was to stop big corporations from conspiring to take advantage of large portions of the American economy, and by proxy the American government.

In further attempts to use federal authority to solve the economic crisis facing the nation, Franklin D. Roosevelt's New Deal established an initiative to build a new infrastructure to be used by the citizens, protected from corporate takeover.

A hybrid entity called the Tennessee Valley Authority was created in 1933 that took the corporate investment structure in tandem with the aim of serving the citizens at large. This was supposed to be the first of many such

organizations, but lobbying groups put a stop to it, moving the United States

into an age of deregulation and consolidation of capital into corporate

monopolies.

After completely outlawing the right to own or trade gold in value of excess

of $100 with Executive order 6102, the Gold Reserve Act took the gold from

US citizens and put it in a national reserve to theoretically prevent the

economy from collapsing again. When the US government took the gold and

subsequently fixed the price, they were able to raise the value of their assets

to recover losses during the depression. But while the short term effects

shored up losses, the long term effects would send the United States down a

path toward legislation backed oligarchy and corporate conglomerates that

took advantage of the deregulation and created a culture of crony capitalism.

As we move into the next chapters, we'll see this cycle of consolidation,

regulation, and deregulation repeat in the modern era, as the Glass Steagall

act faced repeal, and the banks once again used consolidation of

infrastructure to take hold over the American people.

We'll look at how ethics started to become part of the public dialog, and how

the corporate models were dependent upon ethics being ignored. As

information has become more available, the consequences of unethical behaviors and practices have become more public, and we will see how the

Crypto Rush has the potential to be one of the first global economic shifts

that is rooted in ethical awareness, and the implications of such a worldwide

movement based around the ideals of symbiotic existence, practical

application of new technology, and mutually beneficial usage of resources.

Chapter 7 - Back To The Future: Boom, Bust, Rinse, Repeat

Previously, the Gold Rush was used as a historical parallel

to show the potential growth that can happen in a society

with a free market and a sudden injection of capital. This

historical precedent was not only appropriate to show the

potential of new capital, but it also shows the potential

mistakes that can be made from too much or too little

regulation.

Capital can make Barons or Warlords

Money never regulates itself

It's impossible to determine true causative relationships on a macro-economic scale. But there are still clear connections that can be made on this scale that have enough evidence to support retrospective assertion of a direct relationship.

In this chapter, we will step forward through time, starting at the end of the Great Depression, and end at the government imposed dissolution of the monopolized conglomerates that had formed in a new era of a loosely regulated economy.

The regulatory period post Great Depression is a perfect historical precedent to show how the regulation of crypto-currencies could either spell the end of the new technology, or prevent massive exploitation of individuals and organizations.

In modern society it seems impossible to have absolutely no regulation of

Bitcoin, as many governments have shown they will not allow Bitcoin to exist without imposing their rules. In the face of this reality, the special interests of the US, Chinese, and Russian governments and their respective central banks seem to be threatened by the mere existence of Bitcoin.

With the world's major superpowers threatening to legislate the banning or extreme taxation of cryptocurrencies and the recent joint effort of the Department of Justice and banks nationwide called Operation Choke Point, it could be reasoned based on historical precedent that the legislation in a nearly free market with new capital injection will have the new capital forcibly transferred to the state under threat of fine or jail time using ethical grounds as the driving force behind the laws.

In a previous chapter, we talked about the legislation in which the US government made owning more than $100 worth of gold illegal. This forcible removal of capital was said to have been for the greater good of the state, but history shows the overall benefit from this redistribution of wealth was short lived, as the government needed to immediately bolster a failing economy with the Works Progress Administration which established the government as the largest employer in the country.

While the government sanctioned theft of gold from the citizens was clearly a misuse of regulation, it cannot be ignored that at the turn of the century, major conglomerates were using unethical practices such as child labor, sweatshops, undervalued scrips as compensation, and complete disregard for worker safety to such an extreme that the nation demanded intervention. Although labor unions in America had formed in the mid-19th century, it was not until the early to late 20th century that they gained more traction and their influence over trade practices became strong enough to make a change.

During the period in which the New Deal was drafted, the National Labor Relations act came out as well. It was enacted to protect the rights of unions in America. While the WPA may be considered a misuse of funds by some, in the short term, it put government funds directly into the hands of individuals for labor, goods, or intellectual property, and did not rely on the Keynesian principle of trickle-down economics to distribute tax dollars into the economy. While the government was directly paying citizens for work, the anti-socialist movement attempted to establish a hard line between government and private sector, but would allow for subsidies to take place.

The back and forth swing between an unregulated free market and the socialist idea of forced redistribution of capital for the greater good allowed large conglomerates to monopolize industries using unethical practices. As a result the exploitation by these corporations created a political climate in which the citizens were behind a government legislated seizure of the monopolies' capital.

As the American media and communication infrastructures grew into monopolies, regulatory bodies and legislations would be established as extreme countermeasures, to the extent of instituting government censorship on frequent occasions. While historical censorship may not seem to be immediately relevant to Operation Choke Point, understanding how information was filtered in the early to mid-1900s gives a clear example of how government media manipulation precedes forcible redistribution.

During World War I, the United States established heavy censorship around speech and film. On the tails of the war and the First Red Scare, the limits on speech were established in the name of keeping military secrets, and the limits on film were established as film was not recognized as art and therefore not protected by the first amendment.

The government went so far as to establish an Office of Censorship, which censored the journalists, the media, and all communications going in and out of the country. Two years after the closure of the OOC, the loosely monitored Central Intelligence Agency was established as the new agency to control the information flow in the United States.

In the decade following these unprecedented levels of censorship, McCarthyism emerged in the form of a heavy handed government willing to imprison citizens and seize their bank accounts asserting that any American under suspicion of being an enemy of the state was subject to the aforementioned punishments.

As the military industrial complex began to take hold of the government, the clash of domestic interests and international investments came to a head when Richard Nixon once again removed the United States from the Gold standard disrupting local and global economies. Conveniently, the US no longer had to honor its debts in gold, as fractional reserve banking had left the central bank with more debt than assets. To pay back debts, the US printed more money and drastically inflated the amount of currency in circulation, devaluing the dollar in the process.

In the next article, we will see the US government turn its focus back towards domestic corporations, and begin a new wave of regulation that would once again decentralize monopolies. We will also examine a major paradigm shift in infrastructure with the dawn of personal computers, cable television, mobile communication, and the creation of the internet.

Chapter 8 - Video Killed The Radio Star: Mass Producing Consumerism

As crypto-currencies gain wider global adoption among merchants, the price floor of Bitcoin has steadily risen over the past two months. It's impossible to know, though, if the wider acceptance is due to the steady rise in value, or due to governments that have balked on threats of Bitcoin bans.

TLDR: When you can't easily trace transactions, you can't identify the source of growth.

Punch: Most of trading on markets is all fake (Forex, bitcoin, etc.)

(Theranos is the best example - or Martin Shkreli, and those are just the ones we know about. It's happening all across the economy)

In light of the uncertainty, merchants and advertisers are looking for new models of monetization in the emerging digital economy.

New studies have shown that internet users don't follow the same trend-setting patterns that have been employed since the advent of "motivational marketing strategies". Since the American economy is in essence driven by motivational marketing, the need for new marketing models has caused a shake-up across the advertising industry.

In the transition into the new digital economy, the demand for new marketing strategies necessitate an examination of the origins of consumerism to understand exactly why this emerging economy could increase the efficiency of production. The eventual transition to a more efficient paradigm could result in cutting consumer costs, reducing waste, and creating an environment capable of rapid shifts in infrastructure. A clear indication of this transition can be seen in the closing of so called "big box" stores across the nation and a shift towards digital store-fronts with overnight delivery.

It's important to point out that after the "Efficiency Movement", there was a marked and concerted effort to utilize consumerism as the basis for the structure of the American Economy. The most dramatic shift can be seen when advertising agencies started employing product placement and interruption marketing in broadcast programming . First through radio, then through television, the marketing campaigns directed towards American citizens had undiluted channels of information distribution directly to consumers.

While the early days of advertising were overt and straightforward, the increasing success of tactics based on behavioral psychology quickly skewed the advertising methods towards the more elaborate and subtle methods of suggestion. Early experiments in radio such as the "War of the Worlds" broadcast are marked points of research into public response to media, and as advertising became more profitable, entire research institutes were devoted to the art of marketing.

When network television came about, three networks controlled the market. While the networks enjoyed a period of limited competition, the rise of cable television established a host of competing networks which in turn diluted the original market of the three major networks. The expansion of the market on one hand gave the consumer more choices, and in the process the competition drove innovation within media.

As studios and networks competed for the viewers' attention, they had to increase the quality of their work as the number of choices steadily grew. In addition, advances in technology reduced the production cost for small studios, and in turn the competition for the audience grew far beyond cable and network television. The changing production and distribution models of music and visual media have been evolving with the technology, as long term investments become less desirable when faced with unpredictable and quickly changing trends.

It's not uncommon for a brick and mortar store to operate a digital store-front to increase market reach, but the cost-benefit for small merchants can often be a deterrent from expanding into digital commerce. In the same regards, the relatively high cost of using Western Union, or even Paypal to transfer money or make purchases has poised Bitcoin to overtake Paypal's total sales volume.

The concurrent development of payment options with lower fees and internet stores that have world-wide delivery have allowed consumers to have more choice beyond local selection with better cost-benefit returns using crypto-currency in many cases. The inflationary nature of the USD promotes short term spending, as not to lose value by saving at an interest rate that does not outpace the projected inflation. Conversely, a deflationary currency like Bitcoin motivates consumers to be more wary of spending on frivolous items at the potential of a massive loss of capital due to the possibility of a sudden rise in value of Bitcoin.

In this scenario consumers gain the ability to have more spending discretion through access to more variety and better information, and they are simultaneously motivated to take inflationary money that loses value long term, and invest it short term in a deflationary currency that gains value long term. The potential for long term gain through a deflationary currency not only promotes retreat from U.S. dollars, but also from the consumerism based around an inflationary currency . To the contrary, a shift to a new paradigm makes many massive corporate infrastructures like banks or wire transfer services become a choice and not the singular channel of access to capital or transfer thereof. In the same way that music distribution companies had vested interests in seeing file sharing sites like Napster shut down, central banks, wire transfer services, and payment systems around the world are faced with the familiar dilemma of deciding whether to fight the technology or try to adopt it and exploit it at all costs.

In the next article in this series, we will take a look at the modern period and start to look how cryptocurrency can find relevance beyond the early

adopters through ease of use for merchants and consumers alike.

Chapter 9 - iCulture: Marketing the Individual to the Masses

As cryptocurrency becomes accepted by more retailers weekly, the

infrastructure for mass adoption of digital currency has steadily grown.

 In addition to more merchant acceptance, the percentage of Bitcoin

users who use their currency for actual purchases instead of holding it as

a long term investment has steadily increased. There are many debates

concerning the reason that mass adoption has not happened as quickly

as anticipated, but some of the main debates address the diluting of

resources due to the alternative currency market. The other side of the

debate is that unifying all resources behind one digital currency is

completely contrary to the main tenet of "decentralization".

TLDR: What's best for everyone isn't necessarily good for anyone.

Punch: No one really knows what they want until they see someone else with it.

While the market continues to play out, and multiple alternative currencies are released daily, it has become clear that a sort of "crypto-fatigue" has emerged among bitcoin enthusiasts, and alternative currency enthusiasts alike. The struggle to find the balance between competition and cooperation has become the major wedge issue between self-proclaimed entrepreneurs looking to capitalize off digital currency and what are known as "digital-currency evangelists" who look to spread knowledge to make mass adoption easier while not specifically seeking to capitalize from sharing knowledge.

What becomes apparent is the trouble of having a "counter-culture" movement that gets adopted into the "mainstream culture" is not something unique to technology, but it clearly is a major factor in technological progress. Famous stories ranging from folklore like John Henry challenging a machine at a railroad spike driving contest, to Nikola Tesla and Thomas Edison struggling to achieve mass adoption of electricity represent more than a simple technological shift, but they represent ends of epochs. Moving from manpower to machine power has often created a reactionary group which asserts human superiority above all, and those with this view are often labeled "technophobes", or people who are scared of technology.

In reality, it is not wholly a "technophobia", but often a conflict of interest that prevents adoption of new technology. In the case of electricity, it was the natural gas industry that fought the newly emerging industry for control of a centralized method of energy distribution. Ultimately, natural gas and electricity co-exist in the modern economic landscape, but when a new industry emerges, a competitive climate can often cause innovations to be either absorbed into or snubbed out by mega-organizations, more specifically "corporations".

A recent example that has spurned crowd-funding enthusiasts is the acquisition of "Oculus Rift" by Facebook for $2 billion USD after the project was created from crowdfunding. After over 10,000 people invested in the project, the large acquisition yielded them nothing but "sincere thank yous" and "t-shirts". While it can be debated whether the original investors are legally owed any dividends from the sale to

Facebook, it seems clear that Facebook will receive most of the credit for the project's success. It seems there is a paradox within counter-cultural movements to try and move away from old paradigms, but simultaneously needing the validation of the culture from which they are trying to move away.

Within the crypto-currency community, one example of this would be the largely held desire to move away from the central banking system, and the simultaneous desire to attract "Wall Street" investors to give digital currency legitimacy. On the one hand, the technological innovators want to create new systems to replace the old ones, but conversely they need start-up capital which often resides with the entities whom the innovators are looking to replace.

Another example of looking to old paradigms is the current marketing strategies used by alternative currencies. While some alternative currencies have long term plans, some coins are created for nothing but short term pump and dump scams. The same motivational marketing strategies that are employed by major corporations, are the strategies many times utilized by alternative currency PR teams. What can be known as the "appeal to novelty", is not a new strategy of persuasion.

While companies like Apple have gone so far as using the letter "I" in naming their products to appeal to individuality, the paradox of mass produced individuality has been one that has plagued more than just the Apple vs. PC community.

In the context of seemingly tribal or religious affiliations with brand names, the fetishizing of one's own affiliation and the iconoclasm of any opposing party is an accepted and natural state of most cultures that would consider themselves "modern". Bruno Latour addresses this drastic and pendulous swing between associations in his article discussing this specific cultural habit, or some might call it a cultural trait. In essence, his argument is that what can be called a breakdown in communication causes drastic swings from romanticized association to destructive dissociation. While this is a theory based on historical observation, the often contentious and seemingly tribal nature of the digital currency ecosystem seems to reflect the "culture of factish" that Latour refers to. There is an iconoclasm against "Bitcoin" by fiat users, and there is an iconoclasm against "alternative currencies" by many "Bitcoin" users that desire all digital currency energy be focused on one centralized mainframe. In the inability to communicate, fiat users are having a difficult time finding common ground with digital currency users, and by proxy there is limited capital going into the alternative currency market due to "Bitcoin" fundamentalists ostracizing alternative currencies and pushing for consolidation of resources.

As discussed in "One Coin to Rule them All", one clear issue is the disparate goals among the community itself. Some communities are moving towards more anarchic goals, with anonymity and internet freedom being at the tenets of their movements. Meanwhile, there are many communities taking what could be seen as an "orthodox business approach" to their marketing, distribution, and profit sharing models. Treating these communities as if their end goals are equal is a mistake that many make by assuming all digital currencies are equal. It stands to reason that the population at large is having trouble disambiguating any other digital currency from "bitcoin" because brand name marketing has pervaded for almost a century.

Bitcoin itself has been labeled a "Ponzi scheme" by people who either misunderstand how Ponzi schemes work, or are actively trying to confuse people. One might point out that the most simple metric of being an "organization" is not met by "Bitcoin" as is the same with most digital currencies, so a "coin" itself cannot be a Ponzi scheme unless tied to an "organization". As has been seen with the infamous Mt. Gox debacle, "Ponzi Schemes", an exchange that fraudulently asserts liquidity to take on more investors can obviously be labeled a Ponzi Scheme, but this is not a symptom of "Bitcoin" itself, but of unethical business practices by organizations. This type of fraud is not specific to digital currency exchanges, but it is one of the major problems dividing the community. One side calls for direct intervention with "regulation" of some sort, while the other side desires self-moderation through the design of smart contracts, infrastructures, and organizations to remove the potential for fraud to occur.

One solution that has been suggested is the new concept of "Proof of Developer". First posted by Chris Taylor on June 29, 2014, the idea is that an automated system can give varying scores to developers to show potential investors a PoD score which might give more confidence, or prove in fact a coin has been abandoned by the developer.

As mentioned earlier, the ability to transfer currency peer to peer has allowed individuals around the world to pool their capital towards an idea in which a community has formed around. Much to the same aim of

"Decentralized Autonomous Organizations", the natural landscape of digital currency has already produced many crowd sponsored athletes, charities, and start-up businesses. With new access to crowd-funding possibilities, start-ups like Ethereum and Mastercoin have been able to generate funds for their long term plans by looking to crowd-funding instead of simply acquiring business loans. Whether the entrepreneurs or the evangelists will lead the mass adoption phase of digital currency, both sides are wasting no time with development in attempt to break the mass adoption threshold.

Tune in next time for a discussion of potential futures based around cryptocurrency. On one hand, what will be dubbed "Proto-dynamism", we find a transition away from resource battles into a society that has mastered energy efficiency and focus. On the other hand is not an expected "dystopia", but a culture that moves more towards not trusting technology or centralization.

CHAPTER 10 - PROTO-DYNAMISM: DEATH OF THE MIDDLE MAN

"In very few instances do people really know what they want, even when they say they do."

TLDR: Capitalism will never sell you a solution to get free from it, but it will promise you that solution.

Punch: If evolution exists, there is no final state of the economy.

While that quote may sound familiar, it is not the infamous quote by Steve Jobs often referenced to allude to the "product first, customer input second" attitude that is a major problem with the profiteering approach to trade.

As the eighth and final part of a series covering the American economy from The Gold Rush to the Crypto Rush, the freedom to expound on the historical trends and postulate on potential scenarios inherently has limitless potential, and simultaneously has the bias of the author as an inescapable lens through which events will be forecast.

In this case, an attempt to remain completely objective about events which have not yet occurred will be an exercise in futility, so we will focus on utopian outcomes with the acknowledgement that the author has a positive outlook for things to come.

THE MIDDLE MAN

As the articles analyzed historic trends to try and draw parallels to modern times, one of the elements that can be demonstrably proven as a common characteristic of both eras is the prevalence of the "middle man", which is defined as:

A trader who buys from producers and sells to retailers or consumers.

Historically, an intermediary was a way to either establish a third party trust system, and a way to generate income for a person or company with exclusive access to products or goods. While this system on its own works well, in tandem with the unpredictability of human behavior and greed, the process of using intermediaries between a user and a product has caused tremendous drains on the global economy.

One of the paragons of Keynesian theory, the <u>Nike Corporation</u> have repeatedly disregarded ethics in the name of profit.

While it is well known that Nike continues to use sweatshops to get products at the lowest possible cost to turn around and sell them at the highest possible returns, their lack of ethics does not seem to bother their customer base. This would seem to fly in the face of all things rational, but it's the nature of the market. As many capitalism purists defend these practices in the name of the free market, those who study thermo-economics look at the practices of companies like Nike as a problem beyond ethics.

As the middle man continually drains capital, energy, and <u>trust from an economy</u>, they have the potential to bring entire systems to a screeching halt. Unfortunately, many executives who understand nothing but the principle of buy low, sell high do not understand long term planning or conservation of energy. Whether <u>real estate bubbles</u>, stock market bubbles, or Dutch Tulip bubbles, the "buy low, sell high" intermediaries have repeatedly entered markets and drained them of their economic energy just to move on to do the same to a new market.

SQUEEZING OUT THE MIDDLE MAN

As the cycle has repeated many times throughout history, consumers are finally getting access to new ways to avoid the middle man.

One of the biggest and best examples in recent history was when "Napster" was created to allow person to person file transfers, and thus began the downfall of the entire music distribution industry. While the fight against person to person file sharing was initially led by Lars Ulrich of Metallica, other musicians came out in favor of file sharing, and the band Radiohead even went on to release an album that allowed users to download an album for free or donate. Many years later, the effect of P2P file sharing on the "middle men" of music distribution is undeniable, as the record industry lost half of its sales over a decade.

What can be gleaned from the Napster phenomenon is that when centralized institutions face person to person alternatives, the centralized institution is usually made to look like the worse option. As central banks and credit card companies scramble to understand cryptocurrency and how they can try to control it, major developments in the decentralization of currency transfer have been happening.

As central banks rely more and more on government bailouts to exude their control over the commerce of "Keynesian-based" economies, governments that used the middle man approach are running out of funds as well, and cannot perpetuate the shell game. This is not only a good thing for consumers, it is the perfect storm of centralized debt and consumer lack of trust for centralization.

The consumers that have been exploited and drained of their economic energy by the centralized banking systems will not likely stay with these centuries old feudal systems when faced with a viable and accessible option. If capital is able to freely flow around the centralized systems, they will eventually have no capital to perpetuate themselves, as they fundamentally have no concept of producing anything valuable for society.

THE BIRTH OF THE PROTO-DYNAMO

With the advent of Decentralized Autonomous Organizations (DAOs), the entire process of turning an idea into a tangible item gets taken out of the hands of corporations, and the development becomes an intimate exchange between the crowd and the actual developers. When an idea is presented to the crowd, the ideas that the crowd deems fit get funded.

Kickstarter is one of the most well-known crowd funding sources for start-up projects; but as cryptocurrency takes off teams like Mastercoin, Swarm, and Counterparty have created systems that allow crowd-funding to take on the direct route cutting out the middle man. As these systems are improved upon to create "trustless" infrastructures where there are safeguards to prevent exploitation within a trade, viable options to centralized banking are closer to reality.

If one looks at the Crypto Rush objectively, there have been more technological developments within the past six months than there were for the previous three years. This is perfectly in line with the technology associated with the gold rush, as the first miners were able to easily make money with pick-axes and panhandling, but as the gold became scarce, hydraulic drills and tech more advanced tech became necessary to mine the ore.

Just the same with the influx of pyrite or "fool's gold" following the gold rush, the "fool's alts" have made an entire community jaded to the point of throwing out the word "scam" as if it were a common salutation. In the wild west of Cryptoland, the harsh realities of economic Darwinism coupled with the fantastic possibilities of thermo-economics have created a machine which I will call a "proto-dynamo".

It is important to establish the "Proto-dynamo" as concept that represents an entirely new paradigm of economic infrastructure. The concept alludes to the "dynamo" which is a machine that uses opposing magnetic forces to efficiently produce/convert energy. The principle behind the dynamo is to use opposing forces within the same machine to get a consolidated output of energy. If the new paradigm of "protodynamism" can be represented by an electrical generator, the old paradigm of Keynesian theory can be represented by a meat grinder in which ten pounds of product goes in one side, and six ounces of tasteless sausage comes out the funnel possibly tainted with formaldehyde or some random pesticide that is unpronounceable.

Since this article is not simply meant to take cheap shots at Keynesian theory, we will continue to delve into the necessity of Proto-dynamism. As Marshall McLuhan predicted with his "global village" theory, the growth of mass media has quickly made information extremely accessible to the average individual. In tandem with an infrastructure that allows crowd-funding to bring ideas to fruition as fast as possible, progress of technology that is useful to society will be able to hit the most efficient point that has ever been recorded.

The Arab Spring has been an actual revolution fueled by technology and information sharing that would not have been possible without the ability to quickly share strings of 140 characters. With the ability to share information comes the ability to have shared experiences. What have been forecasted as digital tribes by Mcluhan are the logical extensions of a globe trying to break free of the archaic and imperialist paradigm of nation-states.

On one hand, the homogenization of the public forum allows a space for shared experience which can facilitate empathy. On the other hand, a globalized forum necessitates the coexistence of potentially opposed ideologies.

All that said, the perfect storm of a populace that has little trust for centralized authority and a newfound opportunity for decentralized systems is upon us. It is impossible to know what tomorrow brings, but if we look at history, we have likely the smartest generation of humans with the most access to capital and information. From where I am sitting, the future looks pretty awesome.

SECTION 2

The Decentralized Conglomerate: Digital Leadership, Institutional Memory, and Semi-Autonomous Organizations

TLDR: a decentralized ecosystem in tandem with altruistic leadership will be the most resilient.

Punch: to decentralize, or not to decentralize, that is the question.

INTRODUCTION

- - - -

A Brief History of Decentralization

A leader is best when people barely know he exists, when his work is done, his aim fulfilled, they will say: we did it ourselves.

~Lao Tzu~

TLDR: Decentralization goes back over 6,000 years.

Punch: Time will ultimately decide whether decentralization is good or not.

Decentralization as an approach to organizing human teams and capital is nearly as old as written history itself. By the very nature of "decentralization", it can only take place after "centralization" has occurred. Going back 4,000 years to the earliest days in China when divine right was still part of determining leadership, one can find deliberate implementations of decentralization in the application of managing how people operate. The common marriage of religion and bureaucratic hierarchies established environments in which distributed authority or fully decentralized authority became common. In times when information could not be relayed with the speed of modern day communications, having a unified goal inherently became more difficult as an empire expanded.

Even beyond the nuances added by having mercenaries and slaves as part of an empire's army, the speed of communication made large scale coordination extremely difficult over long distances. In historical examples, the larger an empire became, the rulers were forced to become either more despotic or more democratic. There was no stagnation in responsibility. As territories expanded, decisions inherently affected more populations. As populations became more diverse, it was inherently more difficult to find common ground in political agendas.

To understand the ebb and flow between centralization and decentralization, it is important to get a brief context of the emergence of dynasties in China. The current generally accepted date for the emergence of the first actual villages is placed around 5000 BCE. As the exact date cannot be determined, the approximate time frame gives a relative starting point to show the transition from scattered tribal communities to an actual empire that begins a line of dynasties to perpetually delineate power for a continuous historical record that continued into modern times.

The Xia Dynasty is accepted to be the first true empire that arose in China. As a marking point for the transition between the Stone Age and the Bronze Age, the major advances in development created the foundation for the long line of technological discoveries that were yet to come. One of the major accomplishments of the Xia Dynasty was the attempts to control the flooding of the Yellow River by Yu the Great. After Yu managed to get the Yellow River under control, he turned his attention to uniting the Sanmiao tribes. His feats and charisma allowed him to inspire people to follow him as a ruler, and his rule is not known to have been despotic in nature. He is credited with establishing the system of succession and in turn the very concept of a dynasty. In establishing a feudal system that articulated a ruling class and a working class, the innate power struggles of having an oppressed class would forever become a part of the changing political landscape.

In many ways, the early feudal states were examples of the beginnings of decentralization. As the first Dynasty united the tribes, one of the initial acts of necessity was dividing authority and defining roles. While the works on "Division of Labor" did not come until much later in the West, the beginnings of dividing labor for the sake of efficient production and management of capital were flourishing in the first Dynasties. As the power gradually became more unified over the first thousand years of dynasties in China, what is known as the "Mandate of Heaven" came to be the officially recognized union of Divine Right of Leadership and the role of making law. The inclusion of "Divine Right" meant that the government no longer held authority over choosing the leader in the presence of "Divinity". This provision in the approach to passing down the rule allowed for many nefarious actors to manipulate their way into positions of leadership, but it did not hinder the overall development of the nation.

As the civilization grew and culture expanded, technology quickly accelerated, and many of the most famous philosophers and poets emerged from this period in Chinese history. It was at the end of the Zhou Dynasty that government became decentralized as the capitol city moved and a period of warring states began. The states were moving towards wanting sovereign rule for their individual states, but the rulers within the individual states wanted to claim the Mandate of Heaven. It was when Ying Zheng successfully defeated the other states and united them under his rule to proclaim himself the 'First Emperor' of China. One of his first acts as Emperor was to tear down the walls that separated the individual states, and start to build a wall surrounding all of the territories. While the wall does not remain intact today, the Great Wall of China is what remains of what was once a 3,000 mile long wall. As Ying - now known as Shi Huangti- conquered more lands, he became increasingly despotic with his rule. As the empire moved away from decentralization, the unified front allowed for major advancements to be made in building projects and military operations; but on the other hand the increased need to restrict information and free speech was a side effect of the increased authoritarian rule. It was not long after Shi Huangti's death that the empire collapsed due to mismanagement by unfit rulers appointed solely because of nepotism. Once again, the dissolution of a centralized authority caused the territorial control to decentralize and inherently cause more power struggles.

As the Chinese territories expanded, and the dynasties changed names, the ebb and flow between decentralization and centralization was a continuous evolution that formed a middle ground between extremes. Any time leadership drifted too far in one direction, whether towards complete decentralization or complete centralization, the natural equilibrium became a mix of leadership styles, rather than a complete implementation of one ideology. Even into modern government application, what is often misunderstood as completely "Statist" or "Communist" actually has a complex mix of centralization and decentralization in the actual organization of government entities.

To get a better picture of why the centralized government must operate with some autonomy allowed within the economy, it is necessary to understand the organization of territories. There are three basic classifications of government oversight over a territory: province, county, and township. A further delineation of responsibilities separate prefectures under the jurisdiction of provinces, and villages are relegated to the authority of townships. There are twenty-two provinces, five autonomic regions, four municipalities, and two special administrative groups. China also has five autonomic regions that have equal status as provinces. The reasoning is that these autonomic regions are the homes of the majority of the country's minority groups In the West, these regions may be seen as annexed states that are "under the control" of the Chinese government, when in reality they operate with relative autonomy.

The two special administrative regions are Hong Kong and Macao, which grant them special protections. These regions have their own currencies, passports, and judicial systems. While these separations, classifications, and nuances may be hard for a Westerner to initially grasp, the cultural approach to management and division of labor has been fairly consistent in China in its capacity to distribute power and authority seeking efficiency and a unified goal. In that regard, the problem of an individual looking to overthrow the leader and usurp the head of state role has also been a consistent problem for the duration of Chinese history. The "Byzantine General's Problem" effectively originated 2500 years before the fall of the Byzantine Empire.

In understanding the true nature of decentralization as a natural counterbalance to centralization, one must create a new paradigm that recognizes meritocracy as part of the process of establishing a leader or a system without a leader. In a true meritocracy, the presence of a leader is irrelevant to results. In this situation, we can establish the "Mandate of Heaven Dilemma". This new problem becomes an issue of recognizing that if meritocracy is to be recognized, that arbitrary timing of leader or policy changes do not truly serve meritocracy. In the MoHD, a leader can be replaced at any time with a "better" leader if either the new leader proves herself worthy, or the crowd and populace choose to recognize the new authority. In either scenario, the intentions of the new leader are irrelevant. In this MoHD, the meritocracy will establish a paradigm in which the leadership position goes to the most effective and efficient leader with no regards to morality or ethics.

In many ways, the embodiment of what is desired to be the ideal "free market" would be the MoHD playing out on the macro and micro scale. If local leaders emerged based on merit, and were constantly at risk of being replaced by a "better" official, the evolution of the macro and micro systems would be accelerated. It is in understanding the benefits of centralization and decentralization in addition to the downfalls of both that a new paradigm can emerge to make more effective and efficient use of capital than has been previously known in human history. While Keynesian theory sprang forth in a post-industrialized world in an attempt to expound on new methods of scaling economies, it has become clear in modern times that those theories were formed heavily in favor of the oligarchies that existed in the 1800's and turn of the 20th century. Many post-Keynesian theories have been articulated, but mainstream academia continues to cling to Keynesian theory as the dominant approach to forming economies.

As we see the global markets in turmoil and the European Union on the verge of collapse while Britain postures to exit, it is clear that a new paradigm of capital distribution, production, and management must emerge. Keynesian theory has produced a global market bubble that has seemingly popped, as the news of Britain Leaving the EU wiped $127 billion off the global markets in a single day. In light of the MoHD that has been presented, a new paradigm that emerges and proves better use of capital can either be adopted because it has proven it is better, the populace chooses to recognize it, or in a direct confrontation with the old paradigm it emerges with more resources and capital. In many ways, the concerted media attack on digital currencies and Bitcoin have represented the old paradigm's first line of defense in attempting to preserve the legacy systems that currently control global capital distribution.

In presenting the MoHD, what is occurring in modern times is the merit of the old paradigm is being directly challenged. Whether one points at Bitcoin, Occupy Wall Street, the Green Movement in Iran, or the Gezi protests in Istanbul, the old paradigms that control the global markets are being challenged individually. In many ways, the Keynesian special interest groups have actively worked to compartmentalize the uprisings to ensure that the timing of individual revolts does not snowball into a global uprising against Keynesian theory. In an example, the media blacked out the Green movement in Iran, blacked out the Wisconsin protests that were the pre-cursor to Occupy Wall Street, and is currently blacking out the protests in France that are happening in June of 2016. The global mainstream media appears to actively compartmentalize these revolutions in individual contexts, rather than attempt to link them as a revolution against authoritarianism and the remnants of colonialism in modern times.

While this article is not meant to speculate on conspiracy theories, what is meant to be presented is a post-Keynesian approach to capital distribution and management. Taking the thermo-economic approach to capital production and management, an organization must attempt to become a dynamo, which in physics is a machine that takes one source of energy and converts it to output energy to a receptor. The more efficient dynamos can surpass 100% efficiency and start to produce more energy than they take in, but these are theoretical dynamos based in quantum theory that are not yet attainable.

In the context of thermo-economics, creating a dynamo is an attempt to combine physical infrastructure, political management, and capital management into the most efficient economic machine possible. The machine only pays attention to efficiency and pays no regard to the cogs; meaning that special interest groups have no meaning in the context of an economic dynamo. In this context, maintaining ethical standards and moral common ground becomes a function of the system; digital direct democracy.

The Power of Crowdfunding

One of the major benefits to having a Decentralized Conglomerate structure is the ability for capital to be accrued and used towards a given project. This means that organizations that are partnered into a DC have less friction between their organizations to slow down the movement of capital or take too much of the capital in the form of fees and overhead. In the context of multiple businesses working in complimentary industries, the capacity for organizations to pool money towards development has the potential to accelerate the speed at which all participants reach their desired outcomes.

Crowdfunding is anticipated to surpass venture capital in total global investments into the Fintech industry in 2016. As crowdfunding levels reached over $34 billion in total funds raised in 2015, crowdfunding as an industry is emerging in its own right. As laws are changing to keep up with digital currencies and assets, the landscape for raising funds has been forever changed as raising funds with or without equity shares has become accessible to anyone with Internet access and capital. The reality of the quickly changing market demands necessitate an agile organization that can react to market forces rather than attempting to resist the market in pursuit of following the course of what had been planned with no room for adjustment.

OpenLedger is attempting to harness the forces of crowdfunding and follow the trend of increased crowdfunding over VC, rather than try to fight the trend. OpenLedger has begun hosting crowd sales on its platform to enable businesses to raise funds for their organization, contribute to the growth of the OpenLedger DC, and add to the pool of capital for the DC. To give the platform a unified crowdfunding token, OpenLedger created ICOO, which stands for "Initial Coin Offering OpenLedger".

ICOO was designed to be a token that represents the crowdfunding platform on OpenLedger. As the OpenLedger platform is robust and has many different elements, the crowdfunding aspect is another addition to establish a functional economic ecosystem. Instead of creating an ecosystem that only works for existing businesses and consumers, the OpenLedger platform will be useful to startups and existing businesses alike concerning raising capital through crowdfunding.

ICOO represents more than a crowdfunding portal. As there are many elements to executing a successful crowdfunding campaign, the OpenLedger/CCEDK team have laid out plans to organize advertising, generate literature and content, distribute content over social networks, and assist organizations with the transition to having a digital currency system. As well, OpenLedger will be providing tiered options to give organizations different levels of assistance with executing a crowd fund.

The BitTeaser advertising network is a major part of the OpenLedger ecosystem that will help crowdfunding projects get traction. Advertising is the biggest part of getting attention focused on a new project. The BitTeaser community executes paid placed advertisements on websites and affiliate websites, and in the context of crowdfunding, this service will be used for all projects using OpenLedger to fund their projects.

In tandem with the banner ads, the Obits community will contribute paid literature about a crowdfunded project through the 500

Blogger's Club. The club has been focused on paying writers to generate content, and a partnership with the OpenLedger platform through the DC has added the element of producing content into the ecosystem. The synergy between BitTeaser and Obits will create an environment in which an organization looking to use OpenLedger can get all of their needs met in one place. Establishing a central point for an all-encompassing solution will make it easier for businesses to transition to digital currency systems, and in the process OpenLedger will benefit from the DC growth.

Decentralized Conglomerate Theory

As global banking systems are presented with decentralized

options for securing and transferring funds, the market reaction has seen

the acceleration of decentralized technologies ramp up.

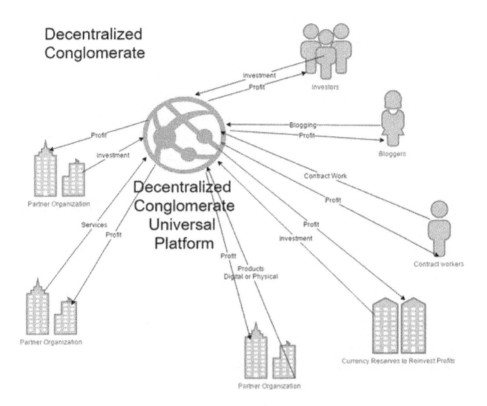

Mandate of Heaven Dilemma

The MoHD is an issue of having a law, mandate, code, or agreed upon

terms from which a "worthy" leader can usurp the current power

structure. The fallout then becomes whether the population wants to recognize the mandate, and acknowledge that by taking over a power structure, the new leader proves herself worthy by default. If the population recognizes the MoH, the edicts and rules of the new leader become law. If the population does not recognize the MoH and decides to revolt against the new leader, the power struggle for leadership ignores the MoH and by proxy the new leader that emerges will ultimately have to give an explanation for ignoring the MoH, or in an attempt to reunify the territories, claim that the MoH was proven by the tertiary leader emerging.

In the context of blockchain technology, the recent failure of the DAO and the resulting identification of a problem with the code of Solidity has established a real world example of the MoHD. What was initially misdiagnosed as a "hack" that drained the DAO fund of around $60 million USD, was later shown to be a poorly written contract on top of code that had a fundamentally flawed approach to its voting and capital distribution mechanisms. In attempting to solve the "Byzantine General's Problem", the coders and system architects were either unaware of the MoHD, or did not give it the proper diligence in researching how it could affect the digital structure.

Effectively, the Ethereum coders created a Mandate of Heaven for their blockchain, meaning if a coder or arbiter could effectively make use of the code or terms, whatever actions they took would be legally binding and technically in line with the protocol. In the DAO "attack", there was no "attack"; effectively an arbiter realized that there was a Mandate of Heaven written into the code and in tandem the DAO "smart contract". In moving $60 million into a "child DAO" following terms and conditions, the "Emperor" effectively took whatever she could and following the MoH to the letter, forcibly removed $60 million from the collective funds.

The resulting fallout has been a mixed combination of applications of theory. While the community has not had a unified voice, inevitably it has fallen on the shoulders of the Ethereum founders and architects to make the decisions necessary to attempt a resolution that will appease the community without compromising the integrity of the protocol. Effectively, the MoH is an agnostic principle that forces the leadership to be efficient with capital, beware of despotism causing revolutions, and painfully aware for the potential of his own removal. The last two aspects of the way the MoH affect leadership are seemingly contradictory, and may explain the common implosion of empires at the hands of draconian and brutal regimes that lose track of effective application of capital.

As well, the leaders that have emerged throughout history as having walked the balance between making effective use of capital and pleasing the needs of the population have seemingly understood the collective consciousness to the point of being able to unify the populations without having them lose their individual identities. In some cases, establishing a new collective identity was the answer to this dilemma, for example in the case of Mustafa Kemal Ataturk establishing the Turkish Republic after the collapse of the Ottoman Empire.

While the emergence of the Turkish Republic did not happen immediately at the end of the empire, it was the unification of the Turkish population against the British in the Nationalist War of Independence, and the simultaneous internal power struggle of the secular republic against the religious regime that had dominated the region off and on since the 14th century that enabled a nuanced government to be established. In articulating "Kemalism", Mustafa Kemal effectively created a "Mandate of Heaven" that ironically gave the military the concept to defend the population from any semblance of a religious monarchy at all costs. While the application of military intervention in a coup d'état may seem completely contradictory to democracy, over the last 100 years the Turkish military has shown that after a coup has occurred, the re-establishment of democratic voting is only a matter of ending the violence associated with the coup. In effect, the less violent a coup, the less collateral damage and fallout necessary to clean up before founding a new democracy.

While the current Turkish government has drifted back near a religious monarchy, the traditional military intervention was pre-emptively deconstructed as Recep Erdogan had jailed many commanders, generals, and officials that would have been the voices of revolt. As the military had become the arm of the MoH in Turkey, the newly emerging Sultanate is establishing a more nepotistic neo-Ottoman empire. While Erdogan seemingly has mastered the Byzantine General's problem by simply "jailing all the generals", in dismantling the MoH he has effectively created a "Wild West" scenario. While there is a semblance of a unified government during the times of the Wild West, the furthest and most rural reaches of what is supposed to have government oversight has no oversight because the government doesn't have the capacity to effectively monitor or secure the land.

One of the nuances of the Wild West is that the most powerful force dominates, and in that regard fairness and humanitarianism go out the window. There are no penalties for nepotism within government, and there are no real penalties for breaking laws in areas that the government can't reach. This is where the world of digital currency has its common traits with actual human history. As digital currency is essentially a digital wild west, having regulators enforce laws in areas that they are not familiar is not only difficult, it becomes questionable if the old laws even apply in the newly charted territories.

As governments struggle to understand digital currencies and their implications, the world of digital currency is "taxed" but seemingly unprotected. The individuals who choose to participate in effect have to arm and protect themselves from attackers knowing that they will get no real assistance from the government that is taking taxes. In effect this wild west scenario breeds vigilantism and necessity for collective response to malicious actors. With the recent attack to the DAO, one of the counter-measures was to attack the original attacker; effectively this stayed inline with the MoH that was created within the Ethereum/Solidity/DAO protocol.

A counter-attack against the DAO attacker #1 successfully secured $7 million in funds from the original $60 million. As the community scrambled to understand the implications of what had occurred, different approaches to solving the overarching problem were being attempted and theorized. One of the challenges facing the community was to decide whether to recognize the original MoH (soft fork and attack attacker #1), or destroy MoH and establish new rules (hard fork and have new genesis block). The Byzantine General's problem has already been failed by the coders of Ethereum and the founders of the DAO in this scenario. The real issue was whether to recognize the MoH or to let the empire crumble completely and free up the locked capital to re-enter into the free market.

The DAO crisis has not yet come to an end as of the writing of this paper, and updates will be made to reflect the long term outcomes of that scenario. It is impossible to predict the outcome of any set of variables, however it is a responsibility of those who control capital to make effective and efficient use of the capital. This requires being informed about the history of capital, and how politics, war, science, art, literature,

education, humanitarianism and countless other variables affect capital.
It is an imperfect science that by proxy the practitioners must continue to
strive towards an unachievable perfection. If decentralization is to
properly be applied in a global economy, the application must be not only
informed, but agile and able to evolve. Reaching a state of stasis is
contradictory to the natural imperative of evolution. In effect, survival is
a matter of constantly evolving whether in the context of nature or in the
context of commercial industries.

Institutional memory becomes an imperative when it comes to
keeping a unified organizational evolution moving. An example of
institutional memory would be "Congress" or the "Supreme Court" in the
United States government. The idea was that instead of having agnostic
principles that were to have authority over a specific set of rules or
actions, democracy would be applied to congress to decide a group of
elected officials that would attempt to balance the desires of the people
against the knowledge of the institutional memory of congress.

In the case of the Supreme Court, the idea is that a group of
officials that are appointed by an elected official to represent balanced
views of the country will also retain the institutional memory necessary to

make informed decisions about establishing new rules and laws. In this context, having institutional memory reduces the necessity of retreading debates and theoretically is an attempt to move debate forward with the knowledge of everything that has occurred previously.

When DAO theory was emerging, the concept of Digital Leadership had not quite been articulated, and the theoretical foundation of the DAO was ultimately rooted in a MoH that created a leaderless system where organizations were to function based around goals and objectives that were agreed upon, rather than the decision of a specific individual or group. Many attempts at creating DAOs have been attempted, with the recent Slockit DAO being the largest on record. While the Slockit DAO was the largest, the success of the project is debatable depending on what metric of "success" is being discussed.

Bitshares token could be considered one of the more successful DAO projects that utilizes a combination of Proof of Stake security with colored coin protocol to allow organizations to receive the benefits of decentralized security, and the benefits of having a centralized currency and platform. The ability for colored coins to be easily converted within the UI for Bitshares makes access to any asset listed on the market equal.

The result is that organizations have incentive to create their own representative asset knowing that there is a centralized platform that makes exchange for other assets easy and cost effective.

Beyond remittance payments, organizational control of capital becomes a new opportunity for capital to become more efficiently used in the context of the global economy. Removing the resistance for capital to flow means that it can go from the least needed to the most needed areas, and in the process generate new capital rather than stagnate against inflation. In the context of thermos-economics, resting capital can be seen as "potential energy", and capital that is being used is "kinetic energy". If the global economic machine is to accelerate, it needs to convert the potential energy into kinetic energy as efficiently as possible.

Efficiency with capital should be agnostic in the global economy. This is where a new paradigm of "Decentralized Conglomerates" apply thermos-economic theory in attempt to create an economic "Dynamo" that makes most effective use of balancing potential and kinetic energy. If a "reserve fund" is seen as a "battery" that turns kinetic energy into potential energy for storage, then creating a dynamo that has the correct number of "batteries" stored away to power the dynamo during phases in which the machine is not transforming any potential energy into kinetic

becomes an agnostic principle that pays no regard to political party,

religious affiliation, or special interest group.

While this ideal state may seem unattainable, it is clear that attempting to

achieve these goals will require a transitional period. During this

transition, digital leadership must be employed to ensure that the capital

does not go to waste. The DAO debacle shows the possibility that

complete absence of Digital Leadership can result in a complete waste of

potential energy with no resulting kinetic energy in the dynamo. It may

be possible that a completely leaderless system is not desirable.

Regardless, the DC makes an attempt at striking a balance between

applying digital leadership and giving autonomy to special interest groups

within the DC.

Final Chapter: When the Crypto-Winter Came

What goes up must come down. Buy low, sell high. Don't go chasing waterfalls. These wise words are all mantras that seem to have been lost on everyone in the cryptocurrency community in what is now known as the "Crypto Winter". In what can only be described as one of the biggest historical losses of value in an emerging market, the crypto-token boom peaked on December 17, 2017 with Bitcoin reaching its peak price of $20,000. The year following was a decline of the entire crypto market's sense of security with Bitcoin eventually dipping to $3,778 on November 24, 2018. Now, many people who might be reading this are saying "But what about the people who didn't invest when Bitcoin was at its all-time high, and invested when it was still $1,150 in January of 2017?!"

It is hard to figure out what provokes media outlets to talk about Bitcoin when and how they do. The media seemed to have been extremely negative towards Bitcoin all the way until mid-2017 when the price really started to take off. As soon as the price showed that it was not going to dip below $1,000 any time soon, the media hopped on board the Bitcoin train. To his credit, Jim Cramer said Bitcoin investors had a better chance at making money learning to play blackjack while everyone else was suggesting to rush out and buy Bitcoin. I am not a fan of his, but he was not a bitter Luddite. He knew the use cases for Bitcoin. He does have vested interest in traditional systems, but those traditional bankers are making money hand-over-fist on Bitcoin via the Bitcoin futures market. "But what about the people who didn't invest in Bitcoin at its all-time high?"

So let's do the math on what a person would have made if they had invested in Bitcoin before the all-time high. If someone had invested $10,000 in Bitcoin when it was $1,150 in January of 2017, that would have bought them 8.69 Bitcoin. As of the writing of this article, that Bitcoin would be worth $47,099. This represents a 470% increase in value. The best performing stocks of 2017 and 2018 were 132% increase and 119% respectively. So a person who would have invested in the best stocks in 2017 would still have roughly 28% of the investment of someone who had invested in Bitcoin. On the other hand, someone who had invested $10,000 worth of Bitcoin in the SAME year at the peak of $20,000 would today have $2,708. That is growth of -%73. In other words, two people with the same amount of money could have invested in Bitcoin with one seeing a %470 gain, and the other seeing a %73 loss. This doesn't even sound right to me when I'm typing it to communicate it to you dear reader. But you can double check my numbers. To quote Lavar Burton, "You don't have to take my word for it!"

If you can't tell by now, I am not one to advocate for gambling on Bitcoin unless you are a gambler by trade. I would consider investing "gambling", sake a few things that set it apart from pure gambling. The differences have nothing to do with the stakes, and have everything to do with the recourse an investor has when encountering a loss. In the case of gambling on Bitcoin, a gambler has no reprieve when taking a loss. In some countries investors will get protection on their losses up to a certain percentage in certain scenarios. "Why, how, and how can I take advantage of this?"

If you think about it, the best way to incentivize investment in emerging technologies is to insure the investment. This is what happens in some countries. I will leave it to the reader to research the countries that do this, as it's not one country. The issue becomes, these laws are often set up in ways that make it difficult for the average person to access the investment pools, and in some cases it's not legal to invest in these investment schemes unless you can prove you have made over $250,000 or have $1,000,000 from provable income just sitting in a bank. Before you re-read that statement: it's not just you...the laws are often set up to make it so that only the wealthy are legally able to pass AML/KYC regulations for investment purposes. Technically, it's legal for someone who makes $50,000 a year to buy lottery tickets in the United States, but they would likely not pass an AML/KYC test to invest in a start-up company.

There are ways that start-ups and individuals get around this legally including friends and family investment rounds, which is basically start-ups begging their families for money when banks will not give them business loans due to them being start-ups. THIS is where people need to turn their focus. The friends and family investment rounds that are in your circle. The next Facebook, Tesla, or even Bitcoin is in your friend or family circle. Every time a person passes over their friend and family that is pitching them an idea to invest in whatever the media is shilling them, they are missing that "big investment" that is actually the big return. The media cycle is too transparent not to be called out on this issue. The media will convince people to invest in a nameless, faceless cryptocurrency before it will compel them to invest in their local circle. They will convince parents to invest in Elon Musk to protect their child's future, rather than invest in their child's business directly. Half the people purchasing this book may have been compelled to do so seeking secret information to get ahead, while the others may have purchased the book to gain knowledge about an emerging industry to get ahead. Many people did this for the sake of their families and their futures. "But what does this have to do with the Crypto-Winter?"

When I set out to write this book, I started off looking at value and from where value was derived. That began a long examination of the history of banking, technology, economics, warfare, psychology, and even how physics is related to all of these things. At the core of everything, the relationships between people and networks that make up societies are the common denominator that drives value. It is not gold, it is not salt, it is not a currency that is the single common denominator. It is people. In this observation, it is relevant to have a human-centric focus in determining the final value of something. In this I mean "How does x,y, or z impact humanity?" This question should be the main focus of finding value. This is not a hippie diatribe. This is an observation of business practices, ethics, success, and failures. It does not matter if a person's motivations are in terms of deriving profit or for altruism if the outcome benefits humans. With this understanding, I want this book to benefit people who want to benefit humanity. Some will be able to make money from the information, and others will be able to use the information to further expand their knowledge set about how humans work as decentralized units as a unit that is not an actual unit.

Too many people were in cryptocurrency to simply make money. They did not consider for a second how either Bitcoin, blockchain technology, or their actions affected humanity. A lot of those people got in Bitcoin before the Crypto-winter and still lost a ton of money for various reasons. Many non-rich average people briefly got into Bitcoin or crypto at the peak due to media influence with the sole intent to make money. I don't blame those people one bit. They are not the same as predatory institutional investors. Those are the prey.

I hope some of those people are reading this and will be better prepared for the next attempt at a media manipulation-assisted pump and dump. Whether it's "Avenger's Endgame" tickets being sold on eBay for $30,000, iPads loaded with Angry Birds being sold on eBay for $100,000, Pogs being hyped as the next "Beanie Baby type collector item", classic cars, or whatever you choose as the flavor of the day; the mainstream media doesn't have to be the original creator of something to pump and dump it. The Crypto-Winter is a direct result of the media hype pushing misinformation cycles that get investors a step behind the person writing the story on-air who has presumably invested before the story about the flavor of the day runs. If you made it this far, I have faith you will never be duped by one of these hype cycles ever again. As well, if you've made it this far I would hope you reconsider that pitch from a friend or family member that you might have passed up to learn about Bitcoin.

Epilogue

Many people might get to the end of the book and not understand the logic of the book until they reflect on where the book started. I wanted to chronicle my journey through cryptocurrency while showing the reader about what I learned in the process. I tried to keep the focus on issues, events, and the least tech jargon humanly possible. Believe me, I kept the jargon down. I wanted to go into the scene with an open mind, and let the evolution of the scene write the story.

One thing that I did not expect was the amount of racism and misogyny I encountered in the cryptocurrency space. The space is not very friendly to women or minorities. This was very odd to me, as originally the rhetoric in the space seemed to be a lot about remittances to countries that had high populations of brown people. I originally thought that the people in the space at large must be awesome if they are trying to solve these world issues. Then I realized a LOT of the early rhetoric was just hollow and vapid rhetoric designed to sound altruistic, but at the core was digital colonialism. "What is digital colonialism?" Well, I'm extremely glad you asked.

Digital colonialism is what happens when a vulnerable population gets "free" digital infrastructure on which they become dependent for some major form of their daily operation. Once the dependency is established, the service is either monetized or exploited in a way that directly benefits the group controlling the infrastructure at the cost of the vulnerable population. What was being presented as a means of liberating the poor of the world was way overhyped in a way that got WAY too many vulnerable and exploited populations' hopes up. Their hopes are STILL up in many places. Now, don't get me wrong, there are a TON of awesome people out there who are doing amazing things to help those people in vulnerable situations. It is not all bad. The problem is, the early days of crypto were all bullshit. It was a bunch of people looking to exploit everything they possibly could. I am not speaking of Satoshi. I am speaking of the people that bastardized whatever Satoshi created. The problem with creating something and releasing it into the wild is that no matter the original intention, the world will shape it in its image. The people that were wealthy enough to accrue and sit on Bitcoin in the early days were not altruistic individuals. These were not people who were out to save the world. They were people out to get rich. The decentralization movement was an afterthought. Don't believe me? Go read Satoshi's white paper right now if you want. It was originally about solving the "double spend problem". It had nothing to do with liberating poor people. The word "poor" doesn't appear in the white paper, and the word "people" appears in the paper literally once.

What was meant to be a solution for peer to peer cash transmission was articulated to be a silver bullet to kill the imperialist werewolf that has been eating off the brown nations of the world for centuries. Bitcoin was never meant to be for the poor. The poor were not in Satoshi's mind, vision, nor white paper when creating Bitcoin. I came to these realizations after analyzing what it would take for people in disenfranchised situations to actually be able to use Bitcoin. I could go through many different scenarios that evangelists will claim Bitcoin has solved for the poor, and they just don't know it yet. 10 years into Bitcoin's existence, and the global wealth inequality gap is worse than it has ever been. Due to the fact that causation cannot be found in a real world setting, one cannot say that Bitcoin "caused" wealth inequality to get worse. However, if the situation had improved, you can be guaranteed some asshole would be out there saying it was Bitcoin that did it.

What I have learned is that Satoshi is the faceless god that anyone can identify with. Satoshi has been present enough to have some character, but absent enough to allow anyone to impose an identity on it without being able to be proved wrong (Except for Craig Wright). In this, Satoshi has been pushed towards disenfranchised youth for them to trust this faceless god over any of their local leaders. These populations have been exploited by many leaders in the past, and the prospect of a faceless god in Satoshi creates an anchor for these people to attach their hopes and desires while allowing them to wholly detach from their local representation. It is the classic cult approach to isolating individuals from their community and family. It's not just you, many of the Bitcoin people have been what can only be called "hypnotized". The issue isn't that they're dumb, it's just that they're in a spot where they're willing to believe that this magical Satoshi person created Bitcoin to "save" them. Where have we heard this?

When I said Bitcoin is "Digital Colonialism" I REALLY meant it's literal colonialism. Part of colonialism is getting a people not to trust their own tribes so they can be more easily imprisoned. Many people will get mad at me for even suggesting these notions. Believe me, I never would have thought I would come to these conclusions when setting out to learn about the Bitcoin space, but here we are.

References

Digital Leadership Definition - http://searchcio.techtarget.com/definition/digital-leadership?utm_medium=EM&asrc=EM_NLN_57771210&utm_campaign=20160524_Word%20of%20the%20Day:%20digital%20leadership_kherbert&utm_source=NLN&track=NL-1823&ad=907917&src=907917

Future of Crowdfunding in Belgium-

https://bolero-crowdfunding.be/nl/news-events/news/financial-crowdfunding

DigixDAO:

http://allcoinsnews.com/2016/02/23/new-gold-linked-digital-token-platform-reveals-crowdsale-website-for-decentralized-organization

Conglomerate Definition:

http://www.investopedia.com/terms/c/conglomerate.asp

Conglomerate Discount Problem:

http://www.investopedia.com/terms/c/conglomeratediscount.asp

Are Conglomerates Making a Comeback:

http://www.omaha.com/money/are-conglomerates-making-a-comeback-berkshire-hathaway-s-business-model/article_a98b99a2-acca-5a89-9108-470d46a3fca8.html

Blockchain startups make up 20% of largest crowdfunding projects

http://venturebeat.com/2016/05/15/blockchain-startups-make-up-20-of-largest-crowdfunding-projects/

The DAO Way: Democratic Investment Fund:

http://www.coinfox.info/news/reviews/5589-put-dao-demokraticheskij-investitsionnyj-fond-2

The DAO Block Explorer (The DAO is a decentralized autonomous organization established April 2016 that invests in other businesses. It is a digital organization with no conventional management structure or board of directors.):

https://etherscan.io/token/TheDAO

Pillars of Digital Leadership:

http://www.leadered.com/pdf/LeadingintheDigitalAge_11.14.pdf

How to be a Digital Leader:

http://www.forbes.com/sites/iese/2013/08/23/how-to-be-a-digital-leader/#133b4ecd515d

Bank of Canada Deputy Governor: Cooperation Needed to Advance Distributed Ledgers:

http://www.coindesk.com/bank-of-canada-distributed-ledger-tech/

Historical examples of Decentralization in Organizations/Empires:

Decentralisation in the Ancient World:
http://blog.richardsprague.com/2012/12/decentralization-in-ancient-world.html

Decentralization: A one to many relationship. The Case of Greece:

http://www.prd.uth.gr/sites/spatial_analysis/ekdoseis-dimosieyseis/mediterranean%20multiregionality%201997.pdf

Ancient Greece:
http://www.shsu.edu/~his_ncp/Greece.html

Centralization-Decentralization Cycle in China:
http://www.vanderbilt.edu/econ/faculty/Wooders/APET/Pet2004/Papers/centralization%20decentralizatio n%20cycle%20in%20china.pdf

China Between Centralization and Decentralization:

http://gbtimes.com/world/china-between-centralization-and-decentralization

Napoleon Bonaparte:

https://en.wikipedia.org/wiki/Napoleon

Decentralized Revolutions that have worked:

-Berlin Wall http://www.nytimes.com/topic/subject/berlin-wall
-French Revolution https://en.wikipedia.org/wiki/French_Revolution

-Egyptian revolution http://www.thecairoreview.com/essays/egypts-leaderless-revolution/

-Fall of the Soviet Union https://history.state.gov/milestones/1989-1992/collapse-soviet-union

Types of Democracy:

https://en.wikipedia.org/wiki/Types_of_democracy

Blockchain Company's Smart Contracts Were Dumb:

http://www.bloomberg.com/view/articles/2016-06-17/blockchain-company-s-smart-contracts-were-dumb

The DAO is Closing Down:

http://www.coindesk.com/the-dao-is-closing-down/

A Hacking of More than $50 Million Dashes Hopes in the World of Cryptocurrency:
http://www.nytimes.com/2016/06/18/business/dealbook/hacker-may-have-removed-more-than-50-million-from-experimental-cybercurrency-project.html

DAO Attacker Says 3M Ether Loss is Legal:
http://www.livebitcoinnews.com/dao-attacker-says-3m-ether-loss-is-legal/

Open Letter to DAO and the Ethereum Community:

https://steemit.com/ethereum/@chris4210/an-open-letter-to-the-dao-and-the-ethereum-community

Mt Gox-style Collapse of DAO: Ethereum Platform Is a Failed Experiment, Says Blockchain Expert:
http://cointelegraph.com/news/mt-gox-style-collapse-of-dao-ethereum-platform-is-a-failed-experiment-says-blockchain-expert

The DAO: An Analysis of the Fallout:

http://www.coindesk.com/the-dao-an-analysis-of-the-fallout/

Proposal: Safety through Standardized Wallets:

https://medium.com/@Alex_Amsel/proposal-standard-wallets-for-d-a-os-a89a4cdcb4a6#.td2rpaivk

The DAO Byzantine Debate:

https://steemit.com/dao/@joseph/the-dao-byzantine-debate

Crisis Thinking, DAOs, and Democracy:

https://medium.com/@Swarm/crisis-thinking-daos-and-democracy-a134b8c721a0#.dlvvv3tgc

Exclusive Full Interview Transcript With Alleged DAO "Attacker":

https://www.cryptocoinsnews.com/exclusive-full-interview-transcript-alleged-dao-attacker/

Simple Contracts are Better Contracts: What We Can Learn From The DAO:

https://blog.blockstack.org/simple-contracts-are-better-contracts-what-we-can-learn-from-the-dao-6293214bad3a#.xyiaycgba

Crowdfunding set to Surpass VC in 2016:

http://www.forbes.com/sites/chancebarnett/2015/06/09/trends-show-crowdfunding-to-surpass-vc-in-2016/

www.ingramcontent.com/pod-product-compliance
Lightning Source LLC
LaVergne TN
LVHW041215050326
832903LV00021B/633